Uncarved Block, Unbleached Silk

For my FRIEND RUDY,
WITH WARMEST THOUGHTS ALWAYS,
JEFF
11/78

Uncarved Block, Unbleached Silk

THE MYSTERY OF LIFE

ALAN WATTS

photographs and introduction by Jeff Berner

A & W Visual Library · New York

ACKNOWLEDGMENTS

I wish to gratefully acknowledge the assistance and encouragement of Mary Jane Watts, Joan Watts Tabernik, Henry Jacobs, Renée Locks, Al Huang and Mark Watts, all of whom smoothed the way for this volume to come into being.

JB

Book design by Jeff Berner
Cover design by Fran Miskin

ISBN (cloth): 0-89104-103-6
ISBN (paper): 0-89104-102-8

Library of Congress Catalog Card Number: 78-53063

Published by
A & W Publishers, Inc.
95 Madison Avenue
New York, New York 10016

Printed in the United States of America

introduction

Alan Watts, the renowned metaphysical entertainer, lecturer and author of more than twenty-five books, four record albums, various short films and an NET television series on Zen Buddhism, made a number of tours to Japan, Thailand and Bali with a small group of friends and fellow students of the exotic insights of the Eastern world view. It was during one of these sojourns that he sat in a Buddhist temple in Kyoto and gave one of his marvellous, extemporaneous talks. *Uncarved Block, Unbleached Silk* was recorded in that Japanese setting in 1970, three years before he left his body in November 1973 at his mandala-shaped retreat in Muir Woods near Mill Valley, California.

I had read many of his books during our decade of friendship, but everything I had heard from him was at the fabulous dinners and salons which took place on the legendary ferryboat S/S *Vallejo* which was his waterfront home in Sausalito, and at the mandala in the woods. So when his son

Mark gave me the cassette of this talk I played it that night in the darkness of my studio. It was around eleven o'clock, and as Alan's incomparably theatrical and gentle voice filled the room, images appeared in my mind's eye from deep space: blowing wild oats, a snail, waves at the beach. Some were scenes I had already photographed and others floated in, beckoning to come "through the looking glass" to form a canvas illustrating, or rather decorating, his discussion of the subtleties of Zen and aesthetics. As the pictures floated I saw a multimedia show and a book taking form, and for a year afterwards I had the pleasure of going on a photographic safari through the "Orient of the spirit" to collect scenes from Pacific Rim landscapes which were Alan's stomping ground for many years.

Alan was interested in visions. He explored the religious implications of LSD in the early 1960s as an advisor to the National Institute for Mental Health, and in his travels collected Tibetan tankas and mandalas of various cultures for visual meditation. Oddly, only two of his many books were illustrated—*Erotic Spirituality: The Vision of Konarak*, devoted to the famous stone temple sculptures of the many positions of love, and *The Joyous Cosmology: Adventures in the Chemistry of Consciousness*, a sparkling evocation of the psychedelic experience. The latter volume is generously sprinkled with two-dozen black-and-white photographs ranging in perspective from a photomicrograph of a platinum crystal magnified 750,000 times to the Spiral nebula Messier 81.

Many religions and philosophies see the visible world as a fascinating, often beautiful and rather tragic illusion. The material world dazzles and hypnotizes us, but "painted cakes do not satisfy." Therefore, the world of appearances is a sticky net from which we must liberate ourselves in order to experience something closer to conscious awareness. Such thoughts have had an effect on my own camerawork. Although I delight in photographing, it is the joy of experiencing those rare moments when looking turns into seeing that makes camerawork a visual meditation. Photography suits this kind of centering all too well, because the camera is a Pandora's box out of which pour billions of images, as if we didn't have enough to pay attention to every day! My personal experience is that the "reality decals" of photography serve as magic windows to stop at in contemplation, or for projecting one's spirit deep into a yonder point.

Alan Watts was a jana yogi, practicing the yoga of the intellect. He rode "the tiger of thoughts and ideas," all the while showing generations the illusory nature of the stream of thinking and inner chatter we find pouring through us while awake and asleep. As with many teachers, authors and "personalities," many roles were projected onto this irrepressible thinker. For some he was a guru (though he scoffed at the idea), to some he was a "Zen crazy," and to many a liberating spirit and prime spark in the American cultural revolution of the sixties. Theodore Roszak, in *The Making of a Counter Culture*, says in part:

> By the time he had reached San Francisco, Watts, who was only thirty-five years old in 1950, had behind him at least seven books dealing with Zen and mystical religion, dating back to 1935. He had, in fact, been a child prodigy in his chosen field of study. At nineteen he had been appointed editor of *The Middle Way*, an English journal of Buddhist studies, and at twenty-three, coeditor of the English "Wisdom of the East" series. Along with D. T. Suzuki, Watts, through his televised lectures, books, and private classes, was to become America's foremost popularizer of Zen. Much of what young America knows about the religion traces back to one or the other of these two scholars and to the generation of writers and artists whom they have influenced.

Watts brought to many the sense that we are all a confluent part of the tiniest molecule and the infinite reaches of the Universe. Here is a philosopher-poet who showed us through both sleight of hand and an erudition akin to the Renaissance spirit of exploring the multiple realms of human knowledge and expression, that East and West have a lot to say to one another. And that beyond the evident polarities of East-West, yin-yang, life-death ...is the high *and* wide human spirit which triumphs not by clinging fiercely to religion, to materialism, to ideas, but by a leap into inner space with open arms, recognizing the "bare facts" of existence while celebrating the transcendental beauty of magic and nature and dreams.

Yet throughout a lifetime of philosophy he often told us with a twinkling eye that if one happens to be graced with an expanded consciousness, the head need not swell up with it! His friends included Aldous Huxley, Timothy Leary, Krishnamurti, Jean Varda, and an international cast of characters from prostitutes to ambassadors. He met and raised cups with some of the "highest" people in the world, and reminded audiences and readers that being truly high includes being truly wide, as, for example, the Dalai Lama, Tibet's exiled spiritual leader now said to be in his fourteenth incarnation, who quite naturally laughs at jokes and weeps at funerals. No stone Buddhas.

Two days after Alan left us, his long-time friend, the poet and filmmaker James Broughton, wrote this poem which playfully incorporates the titles of many Watts books and marvellously expresses the breadth of Watts-san's spirit:

GODSPEED FOR A DEVILISH SAGE
On the death of Alan Watts

He was a gleeful metaphysician.
He loved nature, man, and woman, and their
    joyous cosmology.
He was a scholar and a gentleman who loved
    to take down his hair and kick up his heels.
He traveled beyond theology.
He had shaken the two hands of God.
He understood the meaning of happiness and
    the wisdom of insecurity.
He was a sensual bishop and an impish
    Bodhisattva.
He loved ritual and ribaldry and the ridiculous.
He was a star drummer for the dance of life.
He loved the music of Yes and No singing
    together.
He knew that the only way to hold on is
    to let go.
He knew the way of Zen, the way of Tao,
    the way it is, the way it might be
    and he knew it in his own way
    which is the only way to make it known.
There are those who can dance on a pin and
    those who can pinpoint the dance.
Alan Watts could do both.

I hope that in the following pages the reader/viewer may come a bit closer to the spirit of Zen which is available whenever we pause, look and listen amidst the cacophony of daily events, and enter the "Orient of the spirit" so marvellously described by Alan Watts, teacher and friend.

Jeff Berner
Mill Valley, California
February 1978

Uncarved Block, Unbleached Silk

J want to talk with you this afternoon about some of the aesthetic principles underlying both Chinese and Japanese arts, and the Taoist and Buddhistic philosophies that have inspired them.

In the language of Taoism there are certain expressions used which are the foundations of their aesthetic ideas. One of these terms is "the uncarved block," and another is "unbleached silk."

In the Taoist view of the relationship of man and nature, a distinction is made between the natural and the artificial (although you must be cautioned against taking this too seriously, too literally).

You might say, of course, that the distinction between the artificial and the natural is itself an artificial distinction, because a human building is really no more or less artificial than a bird's nest.   But the Taoists use a kind of art and a kind of poetry which you could call indicative: While understanding that everything man does is natural, some things that he does are "more natural" than others; that is, they look more natural, they go that way. And so the idea of unbleached silk means silk in the raw, raw natural silk. And so in the same way the uncarved block is a sort of stone that would be selected for a Chinese or Japanese garden. (Chinese stones tend, as I see it, to be more elaborate, more fussy, than Japanese stones. And I think that in the art of **bonseki**, which means "growing rocks," the Japanese are a bit more sophisticated than the Chinese, a bit simpler.)

So this rock that you would find
in a Japanese garden is the uncarved block,
or what we call in the West an **objet trouvé**
where the artist instead of making something,
selects it. He finds a glorious thing and
shares his finding with other people, and
that finding is a work of art.

You see, connected with the whole
thought in this tradition of aesthetics
in the Far East, is that superb art is a
work of nature, and not something

imposed upon nature, even though as you have seen in many Japanese gardens there is very complex espalier work on trees and an enormous amount of pruning and trimming done. In fact the discipline of the garden is amazingly complicated and requires a great deal of care. But the object is always, through the discipline of the art, to make the garden seem more natural than it would look if you left it to itself.

It is to work upon nature with skill and craft, but to move in the direction in which nature is already going, so that the uncarved block may be extended into a sculpture. What the sculptor is going to ask the block in the first place is, "What do you want to become?" In other words, along what lines have you already started in the direction of being a sculpture, and I will cooperate with you and bring it to completion.

So that's the principle, really, that underlies Judo. Judo means "the gentle way, the gentle Tao," and it is the art of going along with nature, called **wu wei** or **mu ei** in Japanese, doing nothing, literally not being (because it is man's nature, after all, to act, you can't literally do nothing). To act **wu wei** really is to act without feeling that your actions are separate from nature, when you feel that everything

you do is simply part of the course of things.
Then the way in which you do things is
changed. You wouldn't think so, it isn't
logical that it should be ··· but nevertheless,
if you really feel that you can't deviate from the
Tao, that it lies behind everything that you do,
your type of action, your style of behavior
will in fact be changed, and it will tend to
be in the direction of your seeming to be more
passive than you might ordinarily be.

And the difficulty here is that
Westerners when they hear about Buddhism
and Taoism and this sort of thing, interpret
it as passivity and don't see that what
sometimes looks like passivity is cleverness.
As businessmen often know, if you leave
letters unanswered for a month, when you
return to them many have already answered
themselves. And sometimes when you sit
and do nothing you avoid making very
serious mistakes which might have
arisen if you had acted prematurely. I
have practiced inactivity of this kind

for many years and have always been accused of being lucky, because when I should have done something and been "up and at it," I went and sat and did nothing, and when things turned out all right, it was called luck!

This tendency to look inactive and to go in the direction in the arts of a kind of primitivity we know in the word **shibui**. This quality called **shibui** in Japan is a certain kind of sophisticated primitivity.

Listen to these contradictions, these paradoxes: sophisticated primitivity, controlled accident, where you see that man and nature are really collaborating. Man is the controller, the reasoner, the logical being, and yet at the same time not ruining life by making it all logic and all control. To have logic and to have control, that is to say to have order, you must have randomness, because where there is no randomness order cannot manifest itself.

In the vocabulary of Japanese
aesthetics there are a number of terms
which are basic: The first is **sabi**, and that
goes along with something that rhymes with
it, **wabi**. So often Japanese people speak of

wabi sabi or **sabi wabi** as a kind of mood, a certain art-feeling or Zen taste. And then there is **aware**, which is another kind of mood. And there is **yugen**, and there is **furyu**. Such words designate the basic moods of painting and poetry and so on.

To begin with, **sabi**. The basic feeling of **sabi** is loneliness. One of the great paintings that illustrates **sabi** is the lonely crow on a tree branch. It is the feeling of the hermit, the feeling which the garden artist tries to create when in a crowded country he wants to give you the sensation of being way off in a mountain landscape. So this sense of solitariness, of being able to wander off on your own, is **sabi**, and is something of course which any sane person must have. One has to have privacy, to have space in which to be alone.

It is often thought that Eastern philosophy is against individuality and this is not true. The unity of man and the universe is not a loss or a merging of personality into something impersonal. It is more like the fact that when individuality, when personality is known as an expression of the whole cosmos, then the person becomes individual in a non-strident way, in a way that has in it the spirit of the uncarved block and the unbleached silk. And so one of the qualities of this is solitariness.

The great Chinese poem

which has **sabi** in it preeminently is

"Asking for the Master":

 I asked the boy beneath the pine.

 He says the Master's gone alone herb gathering

 Somewhere on the mount, cloud hidden

     whereabouts unknown.

So the whole idea of Zen is that wherever you stand, if you realize Zen, you will create a mountain. Everywhere is the mountain, even in the middle of an uproar. This is **sabi**. And for this reason then, an enormous amount of the subject matter of Far Eastern painting and poetry is solitude and the love of solitude.

Now there is next **wabi**, which is a more difficult idea. Let's imagine that you are feeling very bad about something, you're depressed, the world is too much for you, you're just sick of life. And then quite surprisingly you notice a small weed growing underneath a hedge and this weed is not just to be dismissed as a weed but is rather a lovely design in the nature of this plant.

Or supposing you are bothered by financial upheaval, wars, politics, and everything like that, and you are sitting on a beach and become aware of the water endlessly crossing pebbles and you get a sense that this goes on forever and ever, and has done so long before you were thought of, long before all human history, empires, schemes and so on. And will endure long after. But something strikes you that is very simple, very ordinary, like the water on the pebbles or like the little weed under the hedge that suggests a kind of amazing eternal reliability of nature that in a very humble form goes on and on. And whatever human beings may do, this everlasting form goes on and on. And whatever human beings may do, this everlasting sanity persists. Now that strange flip from the mood of depression to the mood of a certain consolation in this weed or those waterwashed pebbles is **wabi**.

I'm trying to explain these
things through examples rather
than trying to give you philosophical
definitions. It's better to give
examples than to pin things down
with abstract terminology.
      Wabi comes out in the
familiar haiku

> A brush wood gate
> And for a lock this snail.

This is all there is. The path comes to an end among the parsley, which has a touch of **yugen** but also **wabi** because everyone has parsley in the garden.

Next, this word **aware** is very much
connected with the Buddhist feeling for
the transience of life, that everything
is change and nothing at all can be held
on to or possessed.

This feeling of transience is at the root of the philosophy of poverty that exists in Buddhism and has a curious difference in it from the Christian philosophy of poverty as, say, explained by St. Francis of Assisi. It is like it, but with a subtle difference.

Somehow one feels in the Christian emphasis on poverty that poverty contrasts with richness as good to evil. In other words, poverty is unpleasant but it is something you ought to share with the poor who live unpleasant lives, so if you are to expiate your sins you ought to be poor and to live roughly.

And so for this reason in Buddhism one would not say poverty, but rather say simplicity. Not going without, not avoiding clinging to things because its good to do so, but because it is actually the happiest way to live, because nothing is more terrifying than the state of chronic anxiety which one has if you are subject to the illusion that something or other in life could be held on to and safeguarded... and nothing can. So the acceptance of everything flowing away is absolutely basic to freedom, to being **unsui**, a cloud/water person who drifts like clouds and flows like water. But in this we must not take ourselves too earnestly. Naturally all human beings have in them a certain clinging, so you can't let go totally or you wouldn't

be human if you did. You can't be just
a leaf on the wind or just a ball in a
mountain stream, to use a Zen poetic
phrase, because if you were you wouldn't
be human, just as the person with no
emotions, who has completely controlled
his emotions, is a stone Buddha, so a
person who would be completely let go
would also be some kind of inanimate
object.

So Zen very definitely emphasizes being human, being perfectly human is its ideal. And to be perfectly human one must not have a state of absolute detachment, but a state of detachment which contains a little bit of resistance, a certain clinging still. They say in India of Givan Mukta, a man who is liberated in this world, that he has to cultivate a few mild bad habits in order

to stay in the body, because if he were
absolutely perfect he would disappear
from manifestation. So the yogi, the great
yogi, occasionally smokes a cigarette or
has a bad temper occasionally, something
that keeps him human and that little
thing is very important.   It's like the salt
in a stew.   It grounds him. This is another
way of saying that even a very great sage,
a great Buddha, will have in him a touch
of regret that life is fleeting, because if
he doesn't have that touch of regret he is

not human and he is incapable
of compassion towards people
who regret that life is fleeting.

So the mood **aware** is that touch of regret, of nostalgia, of --- You know that poem that speaks of the feeling of the banquet hall deserted? Here there has been a great banquet, and all the guests have gone home, and there are empty glasses, dirty plates and crushed napkins and all sorts of things all over, and somehow the echo of voices and merriment is still there. And so this mood of **aware** comes up. So even a very great person should feel, because the price otherwise is

not to be human.   For this reason,
Buddhist and Taoist poetry is not un-
emotional. It's not dehumanized and
so somehow speaks very much to us as
people and does not have in it the feeling
that we ought instead to turn into
saints or supermen. That's the humane
thing about this philosophy of life.

The next word or special term is furyu. Fu means literally "wind-flow." Fu is the character for wind. Ryu means flowing, and the dictionaries translate it as elegance, and this won't do.   First of all, remember that the word wind is used in Chinese and Japanese alike to indicate atmosphere, the atmosphere of a place.   So when a person has a certain school of poetry or philosophy it is called "the family wind." That means the atmosphere, the slant, the attitude of this particular school. So that meaning of wind, of atmosphere, comes into the expression *furyu*, and *furyu* is like this: Here is a man fishing and he's sitting in the twilight at the edge of a river with his fishing rod in a lonely little boat tied up by the bank.

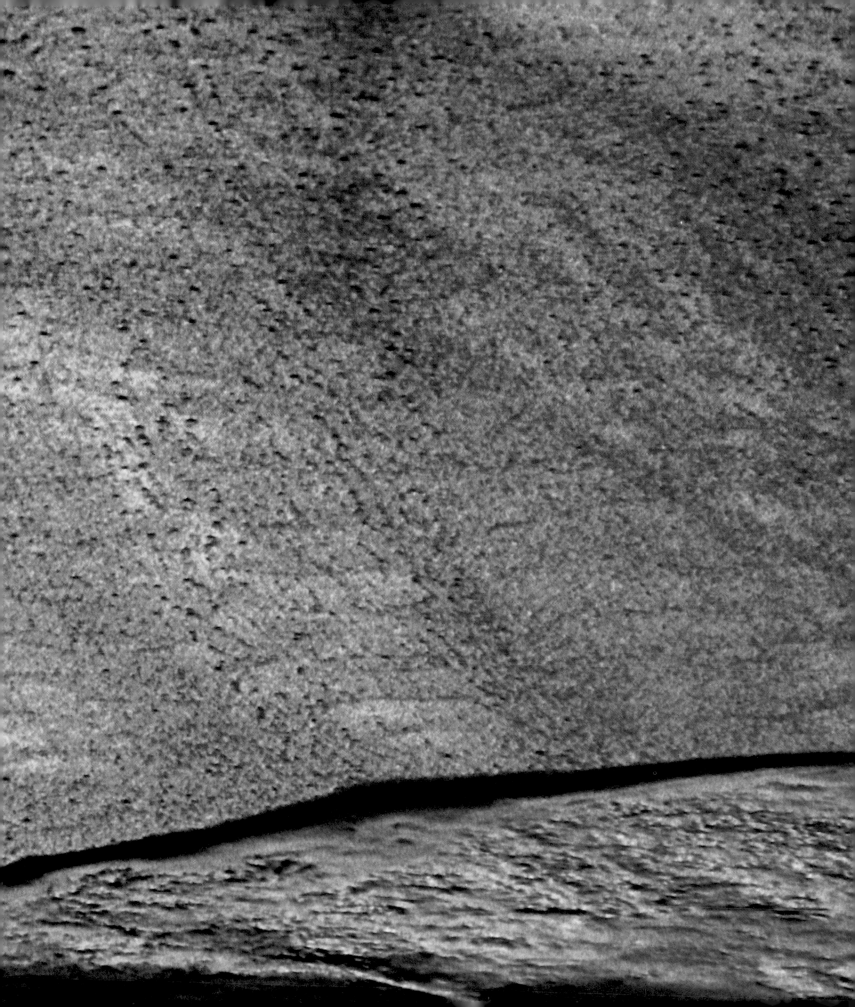

Now if this man is fishing with his mind intent simply on catching fish, this is not *furyu*. But if he is also digging the atmosphere it is *furyu*. To flow with the wind, you see, to dig the atmosphere. American offers the most beautiful possibilities of translation in our incomparable slang for some Oriental ideas. *Furyu* is to get with it, to flow with it, but not in the sense of merely a passive leaf flowing on the wind, but *furyu* has in it a touch of self-consciousness, like the man fishing.

You would think if you studied Taoist philosophy that this would be very bad, this self-consciousness. Chuang Tzu says somewhere that a comfortable belt is one that you don't feel, that you are unaware of. But that's not the most comfortable belt. Would you be completely unconscious of comfortable shoes? No. Something better than comfortable shoes are shoes that you know are comfortable. So in the same way self-consciousness adds something to life. It is one thing to be happy and not know it, and it is another thing to be happy and to know it!

It is like one's voice in the shower room
or bathtub, which has more resonance than
one's voice in the open air. That's why
temples and cathedrals and resonating
boxes for guitars and drums are created
--- to give this little quality of echo, for
all echo is a certain kind of feedback
which enables you to reflect upon
what you are doing and to know that

you know. One might say that ordinary people are Buddhas and they don't know it, and a Buddha is one who knows he's a Buddha. Only they don't let you settle for this comfortably and easily because really to know is also defined as not to know.   In the Upanishads it is said that if you think you know what Brahman is, you have yet some study to be done.   For those who know Brahman do not know Brahman, and

those who do not know Brahman really
know. Now all this paradoxical language
is intended to keep you confused so that you
can't say "I've got it!" So this position
is not one-sided. There is something
about being human and about being
self-conscious that is not a mistake
of nature, not a completely evil fall
into self-awareness. But self-awareness does create all kinds of problems,
because through self-awareness the

human being is in some sense a self-frustrating mechanism: He knows that he is going to die, and the price of being able to control the future is to know that in the long run you won't be able to, and this causes worry and anxiety. But also with self-consciousness goes the possibility of resonance, of realization, of becoming enlightened, liberated and knowing it --- and therefore being able to enjoy it!

So *furyu* adds to the dimension of "going with it." Something more than the mere passivity of "going with," but knowing that you are going. It isn't entirely wrong that the dictionaries have translated it "elegance," yet you could say *furyu* is style. When we say someone really has style, this designates a particular kind of style;

it's the style of what one might call the elegant poor man, the aristocratic bum, the rich pauper. You find that a good deal in the things that we have been seeing. You've gone to many temples where nobody really owns anything and yet in a way they are luxurious. This is furyu.

The next term is **yugen**. The basic symbol of **yugen** is the flower which grows from a rock. There is something improbable, mysterious, contradictory that a flower could come out of a rock.

But *yugen* more than any other of these terms defies translation. The two characters are rather interesting. The first *yu* shows the basic form of a mountain, and then the mountain is combined with characters indicating darkness. You see in the character for mountain there are the valleys, and dark is put in the valley. There is a poem which says "The wind drops but the petals keep falling, the bird calls and the mountain becomes more mysterious." Little sounds emphasizing silence, little motions emphasizing stillness. The quality in the word *yugen* is in the Chinese *Chuan* which means the origin, the deep, deep mysterious darkness out of which everything arises, the depth. In the Book of Genesis we read that "darkness covered the face of the deep," and that "the spirit of God moved upon the face of the waters," those waters of chaos, the primeval blackness which is the same blackness as your head. You know your head appears invisible to your eyes. It is darker than darkness because it's blacker than black. It is practically nothingness it is so mysterious. So when you put these

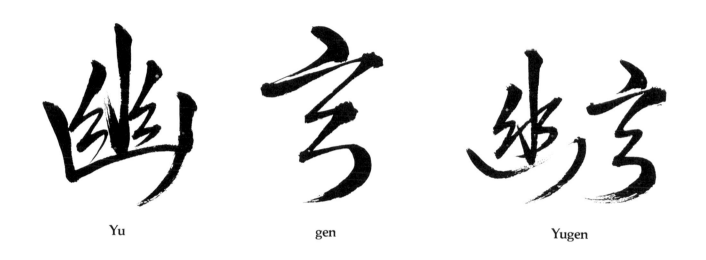

Yu   gen   Yugen

two characters together you get **yu gen**.
And so **yugen** is first of all suggestiveness.
I was looking around one of these temples
a few days ago, where I noticed that you
couldn't figure out how big it was, or
it didn't seem to have any limits.

I said to the priest, "I don't know whether I'm going exploring or not, or just leave it alone and think that, well, here I left Kyoto and never did find out what was through that little gate, and so what!" Forever there will be magic behind there which I didn't define and didn't draw in. So this whole temple was done that way. All sorts of suggestions of little avenues disappearing, like a mountain path winding up among the trees . . .

because always, every wall of a room
seemed to be a screen which led to something
else beyond, and at the back of every garden
there seemed to be a little gate that led
to some other courtyard and everything
led into something else.

Where does it go? True, if you follow it
you will eventually go up out of Kyoto
and get down to Otsu and find yourself
back down in the suburbs. But there
is a sense that the disappearing
mountain path goes to the place that
everybody has in the back of their minds

as the image of the place that you want
to go to (not really an image, as it's
always slightly indefinite). There
is a certain feeling that there ought to
be somewhere that thing I've always
wanted. We get disappointed, of
course, because as we get older we
feel that perhaps it doesn't exist at
all, that one just has to put up with
the second best or something; that
half a loaf is better than no bread,

but still I find that Far Eastern art is very, very full of hints about what is sometimes called horizon.

Horizon is the magical island
somewhere out in the Pacific which
is the Paradise island, and all these
Chinese paintings of wonderful
floating pagodas and terraces with

scholars sitting around drinking wine and so on, are hints of the paradise world, and that somewhere these little steps lead up to that thing. And you've seen these steps. Japan is full of them. As you go along on the train you look up the hills and there are arches, torries, steps disappearing into the hills, all of which suggest the feeling that somewhere out there is that thing.

So **yugen**, as it were, comes around full circle to **sabi**, the wonderful, lonely place at the end of the road where there won't be any in-laws to bother you, any of that sort of dreadful, social difficulty ... but solitude which befits a bearded, old gentleman.

Now of course all these things
are symbols. On one level they are very
human and they reflect our perhaps
childish and immature desires to be
really alone, to have that paradise
thing. And realistic people say, well,

you ought not to bother yourself or
fool yourself with such fantasies . And
nowadays I find that we feel a bit
guilty about thinking of paradise or
horizon or whatever it is, the enchanted
garden. We think, no, reality is what
we read about in the papers and you
have to face it and everything is unpleasant.

(There is the hard-boiled school of zoologists who insist that birds hate flying! You know everyone has always envied a bird and wanted to be able to glide along on wings, and there comes along somebody who is usually some wretched academician who says no, we have discovered by measurement that birds loathe flying. I'm sure they feel very satisfied because they have smashed an ideal. "Oh, for the wings of a dove, far away would I roam, and in the wilderness build me a nest and remain there forever at rest."   I'm quoting the Psalms, but apparently doves just hate this chore of flying!)

It is ridiculous to try to be so
inhuman as never to feel any regrets
about the passing of time and of life. It
is likewise inhuman not to have the
paradise fantasy of the mysterious
place around the corner, just over the
crest of the hill, just behind the island
in the distance.

Because that place is really the big joke:
that's you! That's why you have found that
at the end of the line, when you get through
the last tory and up the last stairway,
you are likely to be confronted with a
mirror. And so everybody is seeking,

seeking, seeking for that thing that you've just got to have. Well you've got it! But nobody's going to believe this, but there it is, the real thing that you are is the paradise land that you are looking for at the end of the line.

And it is far, far more reliable than any kind of external scene which you could love and cling to and hold on to.   But of course the whole fascination of life is that that seems perfectly incredible.

So I think these terms are the crucial ones.   Let me repeat them briefly:

You've got first the uncarved block and the unbleached silk. These are prototypes.

Then you have **sabi**,
the mood of solitariness.   And **wabi**,
the flip from disillusion with everything
to the sudden recognition of how faithful
the weeds are, how the sparrows

chirping in the eves suddenly take
your mind away from important
and dreadful business.

And **aware**,

the regret of the passing of life which

somehow makes that very passing

beautiful.

And there is **furyu**, getting with it and living with style... that is to say, rich poverty, elegant simplicity, the aesthetic equivalent of, well, let me put it this way:

There was a philosopher, van der Loo, who once said that the mystery of life is not a problem to be solved but a reality to be experienced.

That is **yugen**.

And that mystery, that deep, deep,ever so deep thin

nich is before all worlds, is you, the unrecognized self.

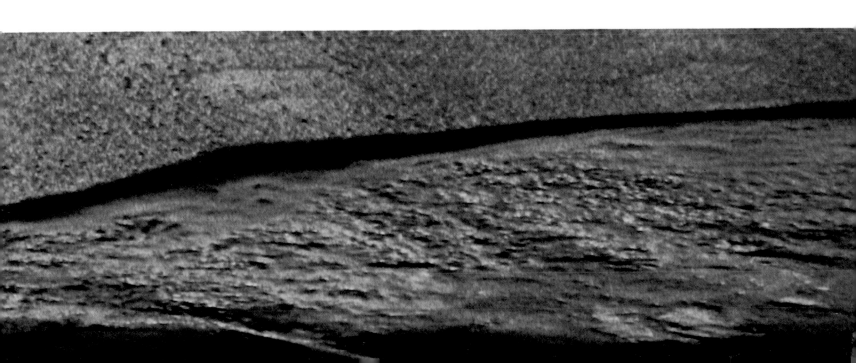